# MEMORIES OF MY DAYS
# AS A BLACK
# CIVIL WAR REENACTOR

# MEMORIES OF MY DAYS AS A BLACK CIVIL WAR REENACTOR

With the Thirty-third United States Colored Troop and Battery B
Second United States Colored Light Artillery Regiment

JAMES E. WHITE SR.

Printed in the United States of America by
One Communications LLC 800-621-2556

# ACKNOWLEDGMENT

THE author wishes to express his gratitude to several persons who contributed time and effort to ensure the completion of this book. He is indebted to Marvin Nicholson, Fred Johnson Sr., Charles Allison, Joseph "Jo-Jo" White, and Charles Willis, for their service as members of Battery B from the beginning. Gratitude is also due to Adam Battery, all USCT, Alfredia Cobia, and the entire reenactor family that sends me pictures and invites me to their events. Cheryl, James Jr., and John Galloway deserve a special note of thanks for their patience and kind assistance with reading and making suggestions.

# INTRODUCTION

I hope the reader will find this book entertaining and informative in some way. This book is intended to do justice to the small group of black reenactors who keep the image of black soldiers who fought in the American Civil War alive. I intend, through this book, that the reader knows that blacks contributed a lot during the Civil War, and through reenacting and living history we can educate the public about the role and hardships imposed on the black soldiers.

# REMINISCENCES

## I

The soldiers of the 54th Regiment paved the way for other African regiments, such as this one.

Photo courtesy of the Library of Congress, American Memories Collection

The first time I heard of a Civil War reenactor was on February 5, 1998, in Southport, North Carolina. At the time, I was a clerk at the Southport post office when two young men by the names of Frank Miller and Marvin Nicholson entered, talking about Mrs. Mary Jackson and her picture of her grandfather, Abraham Galloway, a soldier in the Civil War. Mrs. Jackson was a good friend of the family and my aunt's sister in law. I asked the men about the picture that was found in her attic. Mr. Miller stated that Mrs. Jackson thought that the picture was junk and was going to discard it until she was informed that the picture was her grandfather, a soldier in the American Civil War. She contacted several local historians.

Two of those local historians were Civil War reenactors, Jim McKee and Matt Miller. They, along with Frank Miller and Marvin, began the program. Marvin is a black reenactor with the twentieth North Carolina State Troopers (NCST) and the fifty-four Massachusetts company, a regiment from Charleston, South Carolina. Marvin, from Gallivant Ferry, South Carolina, and Frank, a local reenactor from Southport, both reenacted with the twentieth North Carolina State Troopers.

The men were discussing the commemorations of Pvt. Abram Blount and Pvt. Abram Galloway, two black soldiers of the thirty-seventh United States Colored Troops and both with direct descendants living in Southport. Mr. Blount was in Company C and Galloway was in J Company. Both men were buried in the John Smith cemetery two blocks from the post office.

When Mr. Nicholson approached the counter, he asked me if I was coming to the grave rededication for the United States Colored Soldiers. At the time I told him that I did not know, but Marvin would not accept that answer. He told me that he would be back tomorrow with another friend to give me information on the event.

That Friday, Marvin and Matt, another Civil War reenactor, came in uniform. Frank told me both Galloway and Blount were slaves. Blount enlisted in Plymouth, North Carolina, on December 10, 1863, with the third North Carolina Colored Infantry, which was organized by the Union. Soon after he enlisted, he was sent to Norfolk, Virginia, where the unit was redesignated to the thirty-seventh USCT on February 8, 1864.

After the fall of Wilmington on January 18, two regiments of black soldiers, the twenty-seventh and thirty-seventh USCT, entered the town of Smithville (Southport, NC), to begin occupation of the town. Galloway enlisted on March 1, 1865, in Wilmington, North Carolina. After the Civil War both men returned to Southport. Blount died in February 1912, and Galloway died in February 1927. Both Blount and Galloway have direct descendants that are friends of my family, which was reason enough for me to become interested in knowing more about the Civil War and the part that black soldiers played in the War Between the States.

I know that when I was in high school and college, my history teachers did not teach me about the blacks in the War Between the States. I had to find it out through a reenactment unit. Marvin and I talked for about thirty minutes about the important roles blacks played in the Civil War. He told me that over 186,000 blacks fought for the Union and over 98,000 fought for the Confederates.

USCT STANDING AT PARADE REST

In September of 1862, President Lincoln issued a preliminary proclamation that all slaves in the states in rebellious states would be free on January 1, 1863. Following the

Emancipation Proclamation, recruitment of blacks began. The United States Colored Troops (USCT) was a regiment of the United States Army during the American Civil War that was composed of African American soldiers.

On May 22, 1863, the United States Department issued general order number 143, establishing the Bureau of Colored Troops, to facilitate the recruitment of African American soldiers to fight for the Union army. The USCT regiments, including light artillery and heavy artillery units, cavalry, and infantry, were recruited from all states of the Union.

There were approximately 175 regiments and over 186,000 free blacks and freed slaves serving during the last two years of the Civil War. By the end of the war, the USCT was approximately a tenth of the Union army. There were approximately 2,751 USCT combat casualties during the Civil War and 68,178 losses from other causes. All USCT regiments were led by the men of the USCT and were later used as buffalo soldiers in the west after the Civil War.

## Number of Colored Troops by State

| North | Number | South | Number |
|---|---|---|---|
| Connecticut | 1,764 | Alabama | 4,969 |
| Colorado territory | 95 | Arkansas | 5,526 |
| Delaware | 954 | Florida | 1,044 |
| District of Columbia | 3,269 | Georgia | 3,486 |
| Illinois | 1,811 | Louisiana | 24,502 |

| Indiana | 1,597 | Mississippi | 17,869 |
|---|---|---|---|
| Iowa | 440 | N. Carolina | 5,035 |
| Kansas | 2,080 | S. Carolina | 5,462 |
| Kentucky | 23,703 | Tennessee | 20,133 |
| Maine | 104 | Texas | 47 |
| Maryland | 8,718 | Virginia | 5,723 |
| Massachusetts | 3,966 | | |
| Michigan | 1,387 | | |
| Minnesota | 104 | At large | 733 |
| Missouri | 8,344 | Not accounted for | 5,083 |
| N. Hampshire | 125 | | |
| New Jersey | 1,185 | | |
| New York | 4,125 | | |
| Ohio | 5,092 | | |
| Pennsylvania | 8,612 | | |
| Rhode Island | 1,837 | | |
| Vermont | 120 | | |
| W. Virginia | 196 | | |
| Wisconsin | 155 | | |
| Total North | 178,895 | Total South | 93,796 |

Members of the 107th USCT

## From Slavery to Freedom

The schedule of events on Saturday, February 7, at 2:00 pm in Southport, North Carolina, was as follows:

1. Troop procession into John Smith Cemetery from Taylor Field.

2. Introduction to ceremony—Jim McKee (Director, Southport 2000)

3. Song: "The Star-Spangled Banner"—Southport Chorus

4. Scripture and prayer—Chaplain Clifford Pierce (Fifty-fourth Massachusetts volunteer)

5. Song: "Battle Hymn of the Republic" Southport Chorus

6. Roll call of the dead—Fifty-fourth Massachusetts Volunteer Fife and Drum Corp

7. History of the Thirty-seventh USCT—Pvt. Frank Miller, Company F, Twenty-sixth NCST

8. Song: "Amazing Grace"—Southport Chorus

9. From Slavery to Freedom family history—Blount family: Don Frink; Galloway family: Julia Swain

10. Laying the family wreath—Children

11. Traditional spiritual—Southport Chorus

12. Laying the wreath and remarks—SUV  Camp Davis

13. Presentation of SUV—SUV Camp

14. Laying of wreath and remarks—Southport Historic Society

15. Song: "Rock of Ages"—Southport Chorus

16. Observance—Pvt. Joe McGill, Fifty-fourth Massachusetts Volunteer, and Col. Stepp, Twenty-sixth NCST

17. Scripture and prayer—pastor of St. James AMEZ Church

18. Flag presentations—Col. Toal, Commander, Sunny Point

19. Infantry salute

20. Artillery salute—Col. Travis, Company D, Tenth NCST and Reilly's Battery

21. Taps

About three hundred people gathered on that cold, windy day to see the scheduled event. My family stayed during the whole event, which lasted about three hours. After the ceremony I met several other members of the Fifty-fourth Massachusetts: Chaplain Pierce, Keith Reed, Garnet Allen, Terry James, Charles Willis, Joshua Washington, and Edward "Doc" Keith. They invited me to their next event at Fort Fisher the following week.

The battle of Fort Fisher was a late engagement in the American Civil War. It closed the last Confederate port in Wilmington, North Carolina, on January 15, 1865. Fort Fisher was constructed of earthwork with heavy timbers covered with sand and turf, which guarded the harbor on the Atlantic Ocean. Late in December 1864, a joint Union army and naval expedition attacked the fort, commanded by Admiral David Porter and General Benjamin Butler. General Alfred Howe Terry, with 8,000 troops, left to take the fort. The fleet's cannons destroyed the fort's guns, and on January 15, Terry's troops took the fort. Several regiments were of the United States Colored Troops. Of 2,800 Confederate defenders, over one hundred were killed and the remainder taken prisoner. The Union suffered 1,641 casualties.

When I arrived at Fort Fisher, the first things I saw were lots of Confederate flags. I asked a reenactor, "Where can I find the black soldiers?" The soldiers pointed me to the Fifty-fourth Massachusetts camp. When I arrived at camp, I saw Marvin, Charles, and Doc. I asked the company, "How do you like all the Confederate flags flying around?" They stated that the flags represent most of the reenactors' heritages, and reminded me that over 98,000 black soldiers fought under the same Confederate flag. From that day, I stopped calling the people with the rebel flag rednecks.

We sat around the fire and talked about the history of the United States Colored Troops and the roles of black men and women during that time period. Then after about two hours, Marvin gave me his card to contact him about joining the Fifty-fourth Massachusetts.

One whole year went by and I read in the newspaper about an event at Fort Fisher. I took my family and met Marvin, Charles, and Doc again. This time, Marvin informed me of a new Civil War unit that they were forming, the First South Carolina Volunteers, or the Thirty-third United States

Colored Troops. The Thirty-third USCT was organized on February 8, 1864. Marvin gave me information on the unit and directions on how to get to the next meeting.

The last week in February, I met with Marvin, Terry, Doc, and Garnet at the mall in Florence to assist them with recruiting new members for the Thirty-third USCT. That day I started performing as a reenactor. Doc provided me with one of his uniforms to wear for the day. The uniform was very hot because it was made with 100 percent wool just like in the 1860s. The boots were very different because back in the 1860s they didn't have a left or right boot—they can be worn on either foot. We talked for hours trying to recruit and provide new recruits with information on the meeting the following week.

My next event was a monthly meeting at Francis Marion University to meet everyone. I drove the two hours to the meeting where I met the commander of the unit, Buddy, and Gerald and Scotty Jordon. We planned the upcoming events and talked about getting new recruits to join. The meeting went very well, and after the meeting I completed my application and joined the Thirty-third United States Colored Troops.

The first thing I did when I arrived home was order my uniform—it cost $165.00 plus taxes—from Fall Creek Sutlers. The uniform included the hat, pants, shirt, belt, jacket, and the slender. All the leather goods were $89.00, which included the caps box, cartridge box, and the breast plate. An 1853 three-band Enfield musket was $405.00 with the bayonet, the boots were $90.00 and an A-frame tent was $104.00.

## First Battle

My first battle was at The Columns in Florence, South Carolina, on March 4-5, located two and a half miles east off of Highway 327. The Columns, also known as the Skirmish at Gamble's Hotel, depicts an encounter that occurred on March 5, 1865, when five hundred Federal soldiers under the command of Colonel Reuben Williams of the Twelfth Indiana infantry, marched into the Florence area to destroy the railroad depot. These Federal troops were met by a group of Confederate soldiers who drove them away with the help of about four hundred reinforcements from the area home guard.

At 7:00 AM, my family arrived and we met with Terry, Doc, Charles, Garnet, and Marvin at camp. At the time, we had two tents—Doc's dog tent and his A-frame tent. My tent would have made three, but I left the tent at home because my family wanted to stay in a hotel at the first battle. Terry and Doc drilled me all during the morning until the battle at two o'clock. I was training on how to march, load the musket, and follow orders; it was like being in the military during those two days. A good soldier in the Civil War could load three rounds in a minute and march for miles at a time.

The battle started at 2:00 PM. The weather was cold and wet. There were about 1,000 reenactors at the ninth Skirmish of Gamble's Hotel. I met soldiers from all over the United States at that event. There was a replica of the *H. L. Hunley*, a submarine that sunk the *USS Housatonic* near Charleston in 1864. The *H. L. Hunley* was one of the first submarines during that time. After the battle we continued to drill until dinner, and after dinner we continued to drill until dark.

That night we sat at the fire and discussed the history of the United States Colored Troops. I learned that night that there were 163 regiments of the United States Colored Troops, thirteen United States Colored Heavy Artillery Regiments, twelve United States Colored Light Artillery, and seven United States Colored Cavalry that fought in the Civil War. Also, General David Hunter at Hilton Head, South

Carolina, organized the Thirty-third USCT, which we portray, in the department of the south in May 1862.

The first effort to form a black regiment met with failure initially, due to significant causes: first, Hunt had not received authorization from the War Department in Washington allowing the information of black units, and second, the recruits were involuntarily inducted into the regiment in a manner reminiscent of their days as slaves. After learning more about the Thirty-third and other black regiments, Doc suggested that I watch the movie *Glory*, about the Fifty-fourth Massachusetts Infantry Regiment, which was formed of freemen up north.

I left camp about 8:00 PM that night to prepare for the next day. On Sunday we marched for two hours with the brigade before the battle. Then we had a chance to get a bite to eat. Garnet was at the camp preparing lunch for our unit.

Back in the Civil War, most soldiers ate hardtack or johnnycake: a very hard biscuit made with flour, salt, and oil. Some of the other food items that soldiers received were salt pork, fresh or salted beef, coffee, sugar, salt, vinegar, dried fruit, and dried vegetables. The meat was poorly preserved; the soldiers would refer to it as "salt horse." Sometime they would receive fresh vegetables such as carrots and potatoes.

During the battle, I was able to get about two rounds off in a minute. That was good for my first battle. Later that day after the battle, Doc demonstrated how to keep my musket clean, and showed me several ways to take care of the uniform and gear. Afterward, as we said our good-byes, a movie producer came over and asked the unit to participate in a PBS documentary entitled *The Far by Faith*, which would be shot on location at Bentonville, North Carolina. The unit agreed to participate in the movie.

Every month I attended the meetings and learned more about our ancestors in the Civil War.

# Battle of Bentonville

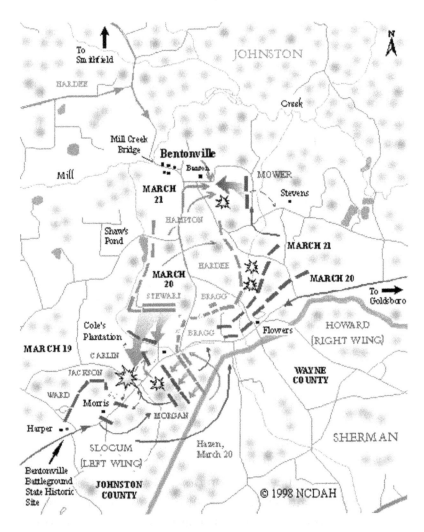

The Battle of Bentonville was fought March 19–21, 1865. It was the last full-scale action of the Civil War. This major battle, the largest ever fought in North Carolina, was the last major battle in that state during the Civil War. It was the only significant attempt to defeat the large Union army of General William T. Sherman during its march through the

Carolinas in the spring of 1865. The next day, Sherman's men attacked the Rebel left flank. They were repulsed, and the line remained static until night, when Johnston pulled back toward Smithfield. The Confederates lost 912 and had 1,694 wounded soldiers. Sherman's losses were 478 killed and 1,168 wounded.

The Harper House served as a Union field hospital during
the battle of Bentonville.

On March 19-21, 2000, the 135th Battle of Bentonville reenactment was the largest in North Carolina. We had about seven other black reenactors to fall in with Thirty-third USCT at this event. We meet a sixty-five-year-old man named Fred Johnson who had family members that fought in the Civil War. Fred had all his family unit information at camp. He asked the unit what he had to do to join. The president at the time was Mr. T. James, who provided Fred with all the information and contact persons. The film crew for the movie

# Fayetteville Arsenal

Arsenal at Fayetteville, NC

On April first and second, I drove to the museum of the Cape Fear Historical Complex in Fayetteville, North Carolina. Marvin, Charles, and I discussed the roles of the USCT in the Civil War. This event was my first experience listening to Charles and Marvin explain how important the USCT was in assisting the north to win the Civil War.

This was my first living history with the Thirty-third USCT. I enjoyed meeting and listening to the reenactors interact with the public. I was so amazed by how much the reenactors knew the Civil War. Also at this event we demonstrated to the visitors how soldiers marched, drills, and living conditions during the Civil War. This event taught me a lot about my duties as a reenactor. I arrived back home and started doing my homework, studying what I had learned and preparing myself for the next event.

## Brother in Arms

Carter Grove at Williamsburg, VA

On June 10, the thirty-third traveled to Williamsburg, Virginia, to Carter Grove Plantation to join other American reenactors of African descent who have served in the military from 1775 to the present. The following historic units were there: Lord Dunmore's Ethiopian Regiment (British Army, 1775-1776), Rhode Island Regiment (American Continental Army, 1778-1783), Fifty-fourth Massachusetts and Thirty-third USCT (Union army, American Civil War, 1863-1865), Terrell's Texas Cavalry, Thirty-fourth regiment (Confederate army, American Civil War 1863-1865), Ninth and Tenth cavalry (US Army, 1866-1898), mounted troops of the frontier, known as the Buffalo Soldiers, Tuskegee Airmen (World War II, 1942-1945), first black aviation unit, Triple Nickels (555th) Parachute Infantry Battalion (World War II, 1942-1945).

During the day, the unit lectured and provided presentations to visitors. The film crew for the movie *The Far by Faith* filmed scenes at night as we sang songs, prayed before the battle, and talked about our pay compared to white soldiers. I enjoyed meeting other black reenactors from all the United States.

Union camp in Williamsburg, VA

## Juneteenth

Fred and I arrived on Friday evening at Martin Luther King Center in Wilmington to set up camp before the other members of the unit arrived. Marvin came later that day to assist us with putting the final touches to our encampment. That evening we met with several visitors and talked about the roles of the black soldiers in the Civil War. On Saturday, June 18, we participated in the MLK parade and provided presentations all during the day. Garret came later that night and joined us with several presentations.

Mr. and Mrs. Johnson at the battle of Averasboro

## Bost Grist Mill

We were invited to the first annual battle of Bost Grist Mill in Concord, North Carolina, on September 8-10. There were about five hundred total participants, and we marched all day until the battle began. One of our members succumbed to heatstroke after marching all morning in ninety-degree heat and was sidelined until the next day. This was one of the best battles that I was in. During the battle, a cannon fired and caught the battlefield on fire. We had to march through the fire with all our gear.

The film crew was also filming scenes at that event.

## The Battle of Honey Hill

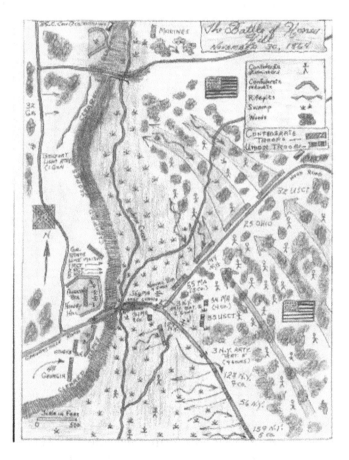

Map Honey Hill 1864

Honey Hill was the third battle of Sherman's march to the sea, fought November 30, 1864. Major General Sherman's main force was not involved. Major General John P. Hatch attempted to cut off the Charleston and Savannah Railroad in support of Sherman's projected arrival in Savannah. The Union order of battle determined that attacks were launched by US Colored Troops including the Fifty-fourth Massachusetts. But because of their position, only one section of artillery could be used at a time, and the Confederates were too well entrenched to be removed. Fighting kept up until dark when Hatch, realizing that it was impossible to successfully attack or turn the flank of the enemy, withdrew to his transports at Boyd's Neck, having lost eighty-nine men, with 629 wounded and twenty-eight missing. Other regiments of the United States Colored Troops included the Thirty-second USCT, Thirty-fourth USCT, Thirty-fifth USCT, 102nd USCT and the Fifty-fifth Massachusetts.

*The Far by Faith* crew continued to film battle scenes. At this event, my wife and I arrived before the other members. We set up my tent and waited for the others to arrive. During the night, we got so cold that we slept in the car. About 3:00 that morning, Garnet arrived. Marvin did not come because his brother had just passed away. During Saturday's battle, the film crew shot some scenes on the battlefield and at camp. The producer asked one of the members to be in a scene on the path talking to Reverend Turner, and I agreed. After the battle, we invited the crew to dinner, and they kept filming while we all ate. They filmed both Saturday's and Sunday's battles. On Sunday after the battle, the event personnel had a drawing and I won an 1860 Colt revolver. That was the first drawing that I have ever won.

## Heritage Farm Day

On October 7, I traveled to Calabash, North Carolina, where I met two of the Bellamy Farm owners. During that weekend, we built a good relationship. I spoke to visitors to the mansion about camp life in the Civil War. Later I talked to the owners and they invited me and the unit to come back the next year.

Soldiers relaxing after the battle at Indigo Farm

The next event was on Bald Head Island, near Southport, North Carolina. Seven of the Thirty-third arrived on Friday to stay on the island in a condo that the Bald Head Association had arranged.

Old Baldy

On Saturday, we had enough soldiers to have a little skirmish. There were soldiers from the Twentieth NCST and other local units. After the skirmish, we interacted with the local residents until about 4:00 PM.

I arrived back at home and began to recruit for the Thirty-third USCT. That was one of the hardest things I had to do. No one I talked to wanted to hear about that time period because of the slavery issues. They did not believe me when I told them the history of the USCT and that the colored soldiers volunteered to fight for the Union and the Confederates. Most people still believe that colored soldiers were forced to join the army, but if they read some of the old military records and other documents they would understand what happened.

## Battle of Secessionville

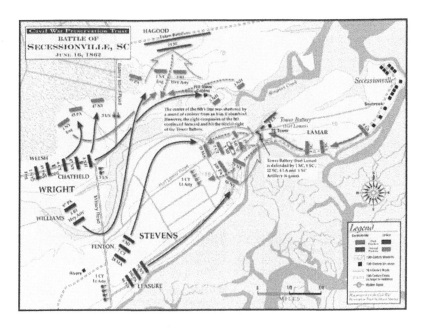

Map of Secessionville 1862

This Battle was called a Union disaster. At 4:00 AM on June 16, 1862, one of Benham's divisions, 3,500 men under the command of Gen. I. I. Stevens, attacked the Confederate position at Secessionville. The attack was repulsed within fifteen minutes. By the time the federal forces had regrouped to mount another charge, General Evans had arrived with reinforcements to bring the Confederate strength up to 2,000. Benham brought his other Union division—3,000 men commanded by Gen. H. G. Wright—up on his left to cover his flank, and twice again attacked the fort. Each assault was fierce but unsuccessful. By 10:00 AM, the fierce little Battle of Secessionville was over. The federals sustained losses of 107 dead, 487 wounded, and eighty-nine captured; the Confederates lost fifty-two, with 132 wounded, and eight missing.

In November, most of the Fifty-fourth Massachusetts joined with the Thirty-third USCT to interact and promote the roles of blacks in the Civil War. The film crew completed filming the movie based on the life of Thirty-third company chaplain Henry Turner.

The following year, the unit added several new events to the calendar, including the Fort Fisher living history program in January. While there, I met two of the staff at Fort Fisher—Leland and Roy. They were very interested in seeing the USCT at the event. We talked about the role of the USCT at Fisher during the second battle of Fort Fisher and the role the USCT played in capturing the fort.

While at the Fort Fisher event, I also met members of the fifth USCT from Ohio. We talked about how their unit plays an important part at Fort Fisher. We talked all day and exchanged information. I did not return the next day, but I kept in contact with some of the members.

In mid February I traveled to Florence for the monthly meeting of the Thirty-third at Francis Marion University. At the meeting, Marvin told the members he was getting too old to march and take part in the tactical. He talked with other members from Adam Battery about forming an artillery unit. Marvin mentioned that one had to attend training on April 7 in Wendell, North Carolina, to qualify for artillery. After the meeting, I talked to Marvin and Fred about getting more information about artillery. I suggested that since Fred and I were the only ones who attended most of the events with Marvin, we needed to attend the certification training.

That following week was the Battle of Gamble's Hotel (The Columns). This was my second year at the event. Like last year, it rained until about an hour before the battle. It was raining so hard, four of us got into a dog tent. That was the only way that we could stay dry. About thirty minutes before the battle, we left camp and marched through the woods and through a stream of water to the battlefield. It was muddy and covered with cow dung.

During that battle, our unit was asked to take a hit by our lieutenant. I tried to find a place that was clear of cow dung because we had to fight on Sunday and I did not want to smell bad all day. On Sunday we had nice weather, and twenty minutes after the battle started, I took a hit and went to sleep on the ground for about fifteen more minutes until the battle was over. I was well rested when the bugle went off to end the battle. After the battle, we marched back to the camp, and I assisted the unit with tearing down the camp. This event was my last reenactment as a member of the Thirty-third USCT.

United States Colored Light Artillery

## Forming the First Black Light Artillery Unit

The idea of a black artillery unit came from Frank Miller, having heard Marvin Nicholson saying that he needed to join an artillery unit because the infantry requirements were getting too difficult for him. Frank relayed this information to Adam's Battery members, and they said that if he could round up as few as six or seven members, they would provide the piece (cannon). The idea took hold and the Second USCLA, Battery B, was formed.

On March 10, 2001, it officially happened at the reenactment at the Battle of Averasboro in St. Paul, North Carolina.
The members who expressed serious consideration were
Charles Addison, Fred Johnson, Marvin Nicholson, Charles
Willis, and me. We attended Fort Fisher and Fort Anderson
events both sponsored by Adam's Battery to observe and to
feel out the artillery.

At the February meeting of Adam's Battery, Alexander's
Battalion, and Longstreet's Corps, we took the part of Adam's
Battery when we dressed as Confederates and our colored
unit dressed as Federals. Battery B was chosen because it
was the first US colored light artillery, formed in February
of 1864, and it had a record of actions that we could use to
impact information about the colored artillery.

At Averasboro, the above names plus three high school
students from South Brunswick High School—Wesley Brown,
Willie Shaw, and Anthony Cowens—formed the first black
artillery unit of reenactors. John Dupree, first sergeant from
Charlotte artillery, had been selected to train us, prepare us
for the field, and work with us on inspection and qualifica-
tion for participation in the battle for the weekend in St.
Paul.

Marvin and I arrived on Friday and camped out with
Adam's Battery and Longstreet's Corps staff members Major
Larry Pittman and Col. Jack Travis. As others arrived, we were
introduced to the piece as a unit. Charles W. and Marvin
were placed in the front of the piece in positions one and
two, and Fred and I were placed to the rear on three and
four. Charles A. and the high school students were placed
on the limber box. All during the morning drills, we learned
to pass inspection. We participated in the two-day event as
the only Federal cannon. John Dupree and the corps staff
members expressed amazement at the efficiency in which we
learned and performed in such a short period of time. We

felt quite special as spectators saw us for the first time operating as the first black artillery unit in the US. The original unit was organized at Fort Monroe, Virginia, on January 8, 1864. It was attached to Fort Monroe, Virginia, Department of Virginia and North Carolina, until April 1864. Later, it was connected to the Hick colored division, Eighteenth corps, army of James, until May 1864, then to Rand's provisional brigade, Eighteen corps until June 1864. Then they were an unattached artillery, Department of Virginia and North Carolina, until July 1864. They were also used in the defenses of Norfolk and Portsmouth, Virginia until May 1865. They were attached to the Twenty-fifth corps, and department of Texas until March 1866. Their service included duties at Fort Monroe until April 1864, and General Butler's operations south of the James River and against Petersburg and Richmond from May 4 through June 15, 1864. They were in action at Wilson Wharf on May 24, and in Petersburg on June 9. They took part in a siege operation against Petersburg and Richmond until July 7. They were ordered to Portsmouth, Virginia, from July 7 until May 1865. Their last service was at Rio Grande on March 17, 1866.

Soldier posted on the gun

## Artillery School of the Piece

On April 7, 2001, I had to travel to Cary for the National Civil War Association, a qualifying school where all artillery units train and qualify for all positions on the piece. All members of the battery qualified on positions one through four except Fred, who qualified on position number four only, with the provisional on the other positions. It was a very hot day and Fred nearly fainted and was removed in the care of a nurse on site.

We were the second trained group for Major Larry P. of Charlotte's Battery. Charles A. was joined by Marvin near Florence, South Carolina. We all arrived by 9:00 AM, and while Fred slept, I drove Fred's truck. We completed the event by 2:00 PM and lunch was served. We spent time with our mentor, John Dupre, discussing tentative plans for the upcoming event at Plymouth.

Before the Battle of Plymouth, Battery B was invited to a memorial service in Wytheville, Virginia, for the John

H. Carter grave ceremony. Marvin, Charles W., Red, Fred, Catherine, and I supported Adam's Battery. Most of us arrived Friday, while Charles, Red, and Marvin stopped at Hoke County School in North Carolina and participated in a period presentation, speaking to a group of very interesting young black junior high school students who were most receptive. They arrived in Wytheville on Friday afternoon, as did Fred and Catherine. Saturday, the event went as planned, setting the piece and firing the salute volley at the ceremony. Rain chased us to cover just as the ceremony ended. I left that Saturday, but others stayed until Sunday. The Fifty-fourth and the Thirty-third also participated in the event, as well as the local Son of Conferate Veterans member.

## Soldiers in Arms

In June, the units performed a living history event in Colonial Williamsburg, Virginia. Black soldiers from every war beginning with the Revolutionary War until present time took part in this event.

Battery B had a high profile participation in the event—we participated in firing demonstrations, living history interactions, and ceremonial firing. We trained as a unit and were the first completely colored artillery unit to man the cannon. Marvin was the gunner, Charles W. was at position one, Charles A. and Gerald at two, Fred at four, J. J. and Eugene at powder, and I was at the number three position. Our commander for the event was Mike Lance.

Even though we were given the highest level of praise for participation and were told to expect to be invited back the next year by the program coordinator, we learned that the event will be modified next year to only include eighteenth-century period participants (Revolutionary War). The reason that was given was that participants of later periods were not responding to the requests, and that the response from the local black community had not met expected responses during the last five years of the events.

Marvin's two daughters and members from his former church attended the event. The weekend also provided the opportunity to interact socially apart from the event. The unit received a stipend of $650.00 and four motel rooms. Fred and I camped out all during the weekend.

## Battle of Plymouth Reenactment/Living History

THE "ALBEMARLE" READY FOR ACTION.

Blacks who were recruited at Plymouth became parts of other black regiments. At the Battle at Battery Wagner in Charleston, the Fifty-fourth Massachusetts Volunteers had four men from Plymouth in the Union uniform. The actual battle at Wagner had 108 men recruited in Plymouth that made up parts of other black regiments in the same fight. About 3,000 of the black soldiers that were recruited from Plymouth joined the Union fleet stationed at Plymouth under various commanders during the Union occupation. They represented a part of the more than 18,000 black sailors, including more than a dozen women, who served in the Union navy during the Civil War. The navy was not segregated like the army, and there were black sailors on almost every one of the nearly 700 Union vessels.

Photo # NH 55510   USS Miami crewmen

The following black army regiments were formed on Plymouth, North Carolina, during the Civil War: First North Carolina Volunteers of African Descent, Second North Carolina Volunteers of African Descent, and the Thirty-seventh US Colored Troops. The Tenth United States Colored Troops and Second US Cavalry also fought in Plymouth from April 17 through April 20, 1864. Forgotten black soldiers in white regiments garrisoned at Plymouth in 1864 include Nelson Sheppard, Twenty-fourth New York battery, George

Washington, Twenty-fourth New York infantry, Alec Johnson, Eighty-fifth New York infantry, Henry Pugh, Eighty-fifth Pennsylvania infantry, John Relic, Eight-fifth Pennsylvania infantry, Henry Johnson, 101$^{st}$ Pennsylvania infantry, John Wyatt, 101$^{st}$ Pennsylvania infantry, George Freeman, 103$^{rd}$ Pennsylvania infantry, Dolphus Garrett, 103$^{rd}$ Pennsylvania infantry, Samuel Granville, 103$^{rd}$ Pennsylvania infantry, Titus Hardy (McCrae),103$^{rd}$ Pennsylvania infantry, Crowder Pacien "Patience",103$^{rd}$ Pennsylvania infantry, and Richard West, 103$^{rd}$ Pennsylvania infantry The result of the Battle of Plymouth was a Confederate victory. The USS Miami was damaged during the battle. The Union casualties were 2,000 and Confederates had 800 losses.

In July, the Washington County History Society invited Battery B to participate in the battle of Plymouth. We had five members to attend the event. Battery B used John's and Roger's cannon for the event. John, Marvin, and I camped out; we stayed up until about 2:00 AM discussing the battle. The reenactment of the Battle of Plymouth was on the very same street that the original battle took place.

We were overrun just as the original federal forces had been overrun. During the day, I visited a house that still had bullet holes in the wall and bloodstains on the wooden floor .The owner stated that his wife's family owned the house long before the Civil War.

After the battle, the local news media interviewed us, as the sponsors, local residents, and media received us very well. We participated in the annual torchlight tour where the lights in downtown Plymouth are cut off and tour groups are led by torch from station to station of activity. Our station was the firing of the cannon out over the Roanoke River in total darkness, simulating the repulsion of the charging Confederates who overran us. There were about thirty-five tours, one after the other, that lasted until midnight. John D. gave us high praise for the efficiency with which we performed under the condition of total darkness. We camped out Saturday and left on Sunday for home. Adam Battery received a stipend of $100.00 to cover some powder expense.

## Blue/Gray Encampment at Kaminski House

Battery B's next event was in Georgetown, South Carolina, on August 17 and 18. The event started with a parade at 9:00 AM. We were an impressive sight in our artillery red, with James Jr. carrying the corps banner. After the annual parade, there were cannon-firing demonstrations on every hour. At this event we had a new member named Darrell, my cousin. We also had support from members of Adam Battery which included Randy, John H., Donnie, and his cannon. The gun was manned as following: Marvin as gunner, Charles W at position one, Charles A. at two, James at three, Fred at four, and Darrell and James Jr. at the powder. Red and Catherine provided the unit with lunch. Adam Battery received a stipend of $150.00 for expenses.

## Indigo Farms Annual Family Day

In October, James Jr. and I arrived and set up camp in Calabash, North Carolina, about an hour from our house. We were the second to arrive behind Marvin. Jim brought the cannon from Oak Island, North Carolina.

We selected the site for the demonstration during the small battle schedule for the last activity of the day because the animals were out during most of the day. Marvin and Fred participated in other activities including milking the cow and a special discussion on tobacco in the Carolinas. James Jr. and I toured the farm and participated in some of the family activities. The coordinator provided a bag lunch. They started with the Thirty-third and the Thirteenth New Hampshire The infantry provided protection for our piece while attached from the wood by the Twentieth North Carolina infantry. Buddy commanded the Federal troops and Scotty the Confederates. Some of the infantry who camped out Friday night had a big fish fry and church service the next morning. All of the members of Battery B left after the event.

## Dedication of the Twelve-Pounder Howitzer

My family arrived in Edenton on Friday, the 13th of October, and set up camp. However, we ended up staying at a local motel. Marvin, Charles, and Red arrived late on Saturday morning. John D., the event commander, chewed me out for the unit tardiness. Also conspicuous by his absence was Fred, who was sick. At that event, I was named gunner of the unit for the first time.

1st Sgt. pushing the round into the tube

We fired demonstration rounds during the official ceremony, saluting the local original cannon that been retrieved and returned to Edenton. During the downtime, we visited a portion of the town and had a wonderful time interacting with local people and eating lunch at a local seafood restaurant. We were well received by the local people, and as always, had interesting interactions with the people.

# Welcome *Amistad* Freedom Schooner

In November, we traveled back to Georgetown, South Carolina, to fire salutes to the slave ship *Amistad.* In order for the piece to be located on the beach, the city employees had to cut the ground piles at the entrance to Morgan Park. Fred towed the cannon to and from Georgetown. We finally got the piece in place after about an hour delay. We were very visible when the schooner came past us.

The prime placement of the cannon and the salute of three rounds with a response plus the announcement and parting rounds were most impressive. The announcement round consisted of Charles W. at position one, Charles A. at two, Fred at three, Marvin at four, and James Jr. at the powder. This was my second event as gunner. At this event, we had Charleston chief Greenburg replacing Marvin at the four position. Marvin later moved to our safety officer beside our commander, Jim.

The infantry reenactors of the Thirty-third USCTs and the Fifty-fourth Massachusetts, under the command of Buddy, assisted as crowd control. Mr. L. White from the Twentieth North Carolina assisted as chaplain, and T. Dillingger of the Revolutionary War and his sons assisted on the powder box. The low country food sampling was outstanding. It was an honor to be invited personally by Captain Pinckney to visit the *Amistad* as a unit. The GPD provided security for the cannon when we were away to the ship.

## African American Research Project

On November 8, Battery B, along with the Thirty-third USCT, was invited to participate in a living history program in New Bern, North Carolina. The unit traveled over three hours to make the trip to Tryon Palace, without a cannon. I could not make the trip due to another engagement. Members that attended were Fred, Marvin, and a newcomer named Joseph Jenkins. Marvin called me and informed me that he arrived with Captain Buddy of the Thirty-third USCT. They arrived and set camp before 10:00 AM. Fred and Joseph camped and talked to the school kids during the day, while Marvin and Captain Buddy answered questions about the black soldiers in the Civil War. After the event there was a stipend of $175.00 to each unit.

## The Battle of Secessionville

This was our second event at the battle of Secesssionville but our first as the artillery battery. My family and I, along with Marvin, arrived Friday night to set up the camp. Fred and his wife came up late that night. Marvin and my family stayed at the campground while Fred, Catherine, Gerald, and Charlita stayed at the motel. The next morning, Marvin and I cooked eggs, sausage, and grits with cheese.

After breakfast, we drilled with the Third US (Adam Battery) until it was time for our inspection. The inspection went well, and we participated in the battle as the first all back artillery unit. After the battle we marched back to the camp. The women had prepared fried fish, chicken, and beans. We invited Adam's Battery and others to share the bountiful evening with us.

Sunday morning we attended the church service with the battalion chaplain. The second day's battle required an adjustment on the cannon. James worked at position one, Marvin at two, Fred at three, Gerald at four, and Jim as gunner. We fired about ten rounds in each battle.

The second day's battle was delayed because of an accident on the battlefield, in which a reenactor got too close to one of the demolition charges. The battles both days had three o'clock starting times, however, because of the long delay, we did not complete the Sunday battle until long after 4:00 PM. James and Marvin had the opportunity to meet with Col. Jack T., Maj. Larry P., and other battalion members (Donnie, Mike, and Craig M.) to discuss the relationship of Battery B to Longstreet's Corps and Alexander's Battalion. We were invited to attend the next corps and battalion meeting in January 2002. Our food expenses came from member donations. We had no registration fees.

## Battalion Meeting

Marvin and I drove up to Richmond in February for the annual Longstreet's Corps battalion meeting. During the meeting, General Maupin discussed the battalion's upcoming events and guidelines for new membership. Adam Battery presented Battery B to the corps for membership. We introduced our selves to several hundred members and they welcomed us with open arms.

Before the meeting ended, Marvin and I presented awards to four staff members: Colonel Travis, chief of artillery; Major Pittman, adjutant; Major Vance, ordnance officer; and Major Shannon, chief of couriers. The plaque reads, "For your guidance, effort beyond the call, dedication, and affection, we are continually in our debt."

During the meeting, Jack and Larry mentioned that they met the unit at several events and that they thought we were a good and well trained unit. After the meeting, we went to lunch with the members of the battalion at the Legends Brewery, a known place for reenactors to hang out, and I had a chance to meet some of them.

## Fort Fisher

This event wasn't on the schedule but since I live close by I decided to go and represent battery B. This year I think was colder that the year before. I stayed at this event for two hours due to the cold weather. I talked to the public about the USCT that fought at Fort Fisher.

## St. James AME Church

On February 10, Battery B attended church services in Lane, South Carolina, and talked to the church members about the role of colored soldiers in the Civil War. After the service, we demonstrated how the three-inch cannon operated. I interacted with the church members while the gun crew demonstrated. Battery B fired about seven rounds, and after firing we were invited to dinner with the church members. We performed for the members that afternoon. We were very well received by the members of St. James.

# Fort Anderson

In February, we traveled to Winnabow, North Carolina. This was the closest event to my home, only about twenty minutes away. Everyone in the unit was present, but we only performed living history because we were without the cannon for this event. We did not participate in the battle. We stayed for only Saturday's battle.

# Carolina Campaign

### February 23-24, St. Paul, North Carolina

This battle was less than two hours away from my house, so I drove there on Saturday. I set up my tent that morning with assistance from Fred and Marvin. The unit continued to use John's and Roger's gun. At that event, I was on the number three position while John was the gunner. We didn't have to cook dinner because the event staff served us. The event was small but we had a good time. At this event, the *Civil War Times* newspaper did an article on the unit.

### Columns, March 9-10, Florence, South Carolina

On Friday when I arrived, it started to rain. I continued to set up my tent before the downpour. It rained all day and night. The battle went very well, but after the battle it started to rain again. Since we didn't have our own gun, I left that evening and headed home.

## Battle of Averasboro

The Battle of Averasboro was also called Averysborough, Smith's Mill, and Black River. This battle was fought on the John Smith Plantation near the city of Averasboro.

### March 16-17, Erwin, North Carolina

In the Battle of Averasboro, we were one of eight artillery units on the Union side. At this event, the whole unit except Charles W. slept in tents. Sunday morning it rained and tents were flooded or blown away in the heavy winds. The battlefield was flooded, so everyone started packing up to leave. Our unit stayed and gave an artillery demonstration to the public. We left Erwin after the demonstration.

## Fort Anderson

### May18, Winnabow, North Carolina

At Fort Anderson, one or two members showed up to interact with other units. Since it was a living history program, most of Battery B took this weekend off to spend time with their families. I attended this event to hear some of the other units' presentations.

## Juneteenth

### June 15, Wilmington, North Carolina

The unit participated in the annual parade and living history program for Juneteenth. All members were present, so we had our monthly meeting during a break in the program. We fired the gun every hour on the hour from 12:00 PM to

4:00 PM. I had several men ask to apply for membership, but they all walked away when we told them what would be required of them if they joined.

I had both of my tents in my infantry demonstration. Most of the kids seemed to be enjoying themselves with the history and seeing the different items. I ended the day by reminding the unit of the next event in August. The unit has one event during the summer because I keep busy coaching baseball, and most of the other events are up north. This event went very well. More people recognized the unit and that we are based here in Wilmington.

## Blue/Gray

On August 17, James Jr. I arrived at the site in Georgetown, South Carolina, about 7:00 AM. We set the camp and waited for the others to arrive. Fred and the other members came within about thirty minutes after I arrived. At 9:00, Battery B and I, with about twenty other reenactors, marched in a parade in Downtown. There were about two hundred people watching the parade. After the parade, we went to the camp-site and fired the gun every hour. All members were present. We performed living history all during the day.

## Indigo Farm

### October 5, Calabash, North Carolina

This was a good local event for Battery B. We met a lot of people who knew us and been following our unit to other reenactments. We had a small reenactment on the island on the farm. We had about fifteen soldiers with one cannon. The battle lasted about twenty-five minutes. The public stated that they enjoyed it.

SOLDIERS AT CAMP AT THE BATTLE OF INDIGO FARM

## Secessionville

### November 10-12, Mt. Pleasant, South Carolina

It seems like every year this battle gets larger. All the members of Battery B continue to come to this event. This year, Charles A. cooked on site. All members participated in the battle. We had two members at the limber box and another was taking pictures. Everyone had a ball during and after the battle.

Marvin enjoying himself at camp.

# Fort Johnson

## December 2, Southport, North Carolina

This event was the first time my mother was able to attend any Civil War event, and I introduced her to Battery B. Afterward, the crew started to drill before the public arrived. When the public arrived, we fired the cannon every hour until about 4:00 PM. This was a one-day event, so after the event we went to my mother's house and ate lunch.

At the time of the fall of Wilmington, several units of USCT were stationed at Fort Johnson. Some units of the USCT stayed for about two years.

## Civil War Preservation Trust annual conference

April 24, Pamplin Historical Park & the National Museum of the Civil War Soldier near Petersburg, Virginia

I received a letter and a phone call from a member of the CWPT staff whom I had met at one of the Civil War reenactment events. She invited the unit to take part in their next conference. During the next battery meeting, I told the unit about the invitation and we voted to participate. Two weeks after talking to the CWPT staff, I called her back and informed her that Battery B had accepted her invitation.

My family and I arrived in Petersburg about 3:00 PM .and started setting up camp. After completing the camp, we visited the museum and interacted with members of the conference until it was time to interpret to visitors what soldiers commonly did in camp. We mingled with the guests until the conference was over.

## Raising the *Hunley*

After years of planning and months of work, the *H. L. Hunley* was finally ready for its journey home. That morning, the *Karlissa B* crane removed the *H. L. Hunley* from the bottom of the Charleston ocean floor to a recovery barge.

The Thirty-third USCT and Fifty-fourth Massachusetts participated in a ceremony to honor the fallen soldiers aboard the great vessel. I was among the color guard aboard the ship with other local reenactors. The ceremony lasted about forty-five minutes, and smaller boats began coming close to the ship. I noticed that there were hundreds of boats at that great ceremony. On the way to the lab, the barge was to come close to the *USS Yorktown*, but the smaller boats were in the safety zone and the barge could no longer come close to the ship. The barge transported the *H. L. Hunley* to the former Charleston Navy base to a specially designed lab.

James and Charles inspect the gun

## Battle of Pocahontas

On May 24, Confederate Maj. Gen. Fitzhugh Lee's cavalry division, with about 3,000 men, attacked the Union supply depot at Wilson's Wharf on the James River near Charles City, Virginia. Two African American regiments of the United States Colored Troops under the command of Brig. Gen. Edward A. Wild, a total of about 1,800 men, were in the process of constructing a fortification there. That fort was subsequently named Fort Pocahontas.

Wild commanded 1,100 men and two cannons. The Union force consisted of the First United Stated Colored Troops and four companies of the Tenth United States Colored Troops. Battery M, Third New York Artillery, was the only all-white unit. The gunboat *USS Dawn* lay in the James River to deliver fire support to the fort. Federal losses included six killed and forty wounded. About two hundred Confederates were killed or wounded in the attack.

Soldiers marching to battle

Soldiers waiting on the battle to begin.

## May 21, The battle of Pocahontas, Charles City, Virginia

My family attended this event with me. We left home at 8:00 AM and arrived in Charles City at 3:00 PM. While waiting for the rest of the group to arrive to help set up camp, we interacted with other members of the USCT. We met members from the Third, Fifth, Sixth, Fifty-fourth, and Fourteenth US colored heavy artillery. They were glad to see a colored artillery unit. Most of the units said that they read about our artillery unit in the *Civil War Times*. We talked for about an hour before the rest of the members arrived.

After the other members arrived we set the camp and started cooking on the grill before night. We had previously arranged our supply lists for the weekend, as the nearest store was about thirty minutes away. My family, John H., and Marvin camped out while Fred and Charles W. went to the hotel. We stayed up until about two o'clock talking and interacting with other units.

The next morning, Marvin and I cooked breakfast. My family assisted with keeping the camp clean and washing the dishes. Everyone arrived just before 9:00 AM. I reminded the members of Battery B that the camp site opens up at 9:00 AM and we needed to be in place. I marched the unit to the gun and drilled on the gun until time for inspection. Everything passed inspection and Battery B looked good doing the dry run on the gun. We received praise from the Eighteenth corps and other artillery units.

I marched the unit back to the campsite to interact with the public before the battle began. Some members were posted at camp while others went to the sutler to buy items. At 1:30, I inspected members of Battery B just before we marched to the battlefield. While on the battlefield, I made sure that the gun tube was clean by placing a worm (a tool to clean gun) in the tube.

At 2:00 PM the battle began with the firing of a Confederate cannon. During the battle, we shot twelve rounds. Most of the time we had to wait until the infantry was in the safe zone. The battle lasted about forty-five minutes.

After the battle we marched with all the other units back to the camp. At this point, the camp was still open to the public, so we continued to interact with the public until the camp closed. We ate dinner with the other reenactors at the waterfront. That evening was reserved for family time and we were free for the rest of the day.

The family and I visited the museum and other campsites. On Sunday, the battle was at 1:00 PM. We started packing up that morning so we could get back home before dark. Everyone at camp assisted and we were finished with the camp around 11:00 AM. We left Charles City after the battle that afternoon.

Artillerymen drilling before the battle

# Juneteenth

The third weekend in June is known as Juneteenth. This year we were invited to participate in the Southport, North Carolina, annual event. Juneteenth is the oldest known celebration to end African American slavery throughout the United States. Communities celebrate the whole week leading up to the weekend. Most communities have entertainment all week.

We arrived on Friday night and camped on the baseball field near A. C. Caviness Memorial Park. The next morning we marched in the parade and fired the three-inch cannon every half hour until 4:00 PM. We had several visitors visit the camp and learn about the times and life of a United States colored soldier during the Civil War.

## Blue/Gray Encampment at Kaminski House

The unit was asked again to participate in a living history program and parade at the Kaminski House Museum. The house was built in 1769, and in 1972 it was deeded to the city of Georgetown, South Carolina. I pulled John's and Roger's gun to Georgetown Saturday morning for the parade. The battery interacted with the public until it was time to fire the gun. We fired the gun every hour until 4:00 PM.

## The Battle of Secessionville

John and Roger were nice to let us use their gun for this event. On Thursday evening, James Jr. and I went to John's house to get the cannon. The next day, Jo-Jo and I, along with the family, left home on our way to Mt. Pleasant, South Carolina. We arrived at the plantation at 1:00 PM. During that time, the schoolchildren were going to different camps for living history presentations.

As we were setting up camp, Marvin and Fred arrived. They chipped in and we had the camp up before 3:00 pm. Marvin camped with the unit, but Fred and his wife went to the hotel. The next day we had artillery inspection in the morning. Fred made it just in time to have a gun crew. Most gun crews consist of five or more men, but no less than four.

We passed the inspection and were ready for the battle. During the battle, we fired thirty rounds. The battle was large, and as always, we were the closest cannon to the public, with ten other cannons on the Union side.

Everyone, including our families, enjoyed themselves at the battle and shopping after at sutler row. This is the highlight for our families because there are lots of activities for the wives and children. They like going inside the big house, the slave quarter, and watching the women make straw hats and other items. This was the last major battle of the year for Battery B.

Every year, Charles A. invites the unit to his home for a big dinner. After dinner Friday night, we headed back to camp and interacted with the other units.

## Fayetteville Museum

During the Christmas season, several members of Battery B attended the museum's Christmas living history program. We, with other Civil War reenactors, told the public how life was during the holiday season. The program lasted for one day. We cooked for the public and invited them to have some of the food that most soldiers had during the war.

## December 7, The Annual Christmas dinner

This was Battery B's first Christmas dinner together. It was at a restaurant in Southport. The entire membership attended, with their families. As acting president, I presented several members with awards. Marvin and James Jr. were both voted outstanding members for the year. They each received a member certificate with their names and a trophy. We continue to have Christmas dinner every year and give outstanding member awards.

Soldiers relaxing before the battle

First Sgt. White conversed with Frederick Douglass before he left to meet with the president.

The White brother First Sgt. meets with Frederick Douglass to update him on how the USCT are being treated.

As the years passed we lost one faithful member—Charles Willis, and a special friend—Frank Miller. Several new members have joined and left. We added several more events to our schedule which include the annual African American Cultural Celebration, the Battle of Fork Roads, the Battle of Locust Grove, the North Carolina Azalea Festival at Wilmington, the Civil War symposium, Fayetteville Museum living history, the Battle of Goldsboro, the Battle of the Outer Bank, the Raid on Ashpole, and several parades in North Carolina in Wilmington, Southport, Leland, Fairmont, and Bolivia. The parades in South Carolina include Charleston and Florence.

One of the medals that the USCT received during the Civil War

USCT MEMBERS

National Cemetery graves of members of USCT